The Life of an E.C.O. in India

The Life of an E.C.O.
in India

Robin Sharp

The Pentland Press Limited
Edinburgh • Cambridge • Durham

© Robin Sharp 1994

First published in 1994 by
The Pentland Press Ltd.
1 Hutton Close
South Church
Bishop Auckland
Durham

All rights reserved.
Unauthorised duplication
contravenes existing laws.

ISBN 1 85821 192 1

Typeset by CBS, Felixstowe, Suffolk
Printed and bound by Antony Rowe Ltd., Chippenham

Dedicated to the memory of
the Late Francis Everard Sharp, C.I.E.,
formerly Deputy Inspector General of the
Criminal Investigation Department,
Indian Police

Contents

Enlisting and Embarking	1
Landing and Disembarking	5
From Bombay to Bangalore	9
Training at the O.T.S.	13
Up to N.W.F.P. and more Training	17
First Posting and First Assignment	21
From Assam to Bengal	27
Work at the Advanced Base Supply Depot	29
Sickness and Leave	33
Return to Chittagong	35
Another Leave and a Long Journey	39
End of War in the East	41
Home Leave	43
Return to India	47
Two Postings	51
Poona and Simla	55
Disbanding of a Unit	59
Home-coming and Becoming a Civilian	63

I

Enlisting and Embarking

When the War began in 1939 I was mad keen to join the Army. I was only 15, having just taken School Certificate, and another three years of schooling were ahead of me before I could enlist. During that time I was in the Cadet Corps and the Home Guard at the same time.

But in 1942, at the age of 18, I left school and immediately volunteered to join the Indian Army.

I would have been 'called up' two or three months later anyway, but as it was I had the privilege, for what it was worth, of saying that I was a volunteer. The attraction of going into the Indian Army at the time was that it was a short cut to gaining a Commission quickly; whereas in the British Army at the time every one had to 'go through the ranks' for at least three months, an initiation that would probably have done one good anyway.

However, I fell for the bait, was accepted by the India Office, and within a fortnight of leaving school was ordered to report at the London Area Transit Camp, a former Railway Hotel at Marylebone, and a week later was on a troopship bound for India.

There were a number of other ex- Public School men like myself joining at the same place and time, together with some enlisted men or British Other Ranks, who had been earmarked for this singular honour of being selected for Commission into the Indian Army. We all enlisted into the Royal Scots, but this was for the purpose of records only. We were Privates for about a week, and then were promoted to Cadets and were allowed to put up white flashes on our epaulettes.

During our week in London, we were fitted out with uniform, both routine and tropical, were drilled quite a bit, had several inoculations, and in the evenings were permitted to go out, provided that we did not leave the London area.

The Life of an E.C.O. in India

At last the day for embarkation came and we were put on coaches for a special entraining point outside one of the main London termini. This we discovered was for security reasons. The funny thing about it was that we on our draft all *knew* that we were bound for India, for that was in our contract, so to speak. But there were plenty of other men on the troop train and on the troop ship who were under sailing orders, but were supposed to have no idea as to whether they were bound for the Middle East, the Far East, or anywhere else.

After a rather uncomfortable journey northwards overnight, we were decanted in the early morning in a shed by some sidings up the Clyde outside Glasgow. We spent a long day waiting to be allowed to go aboard, with dull old army rations being dished out into mess tins from time to time.

As evening fell, we were allowed to go on board. The ship that was to take us out to India was a Dutch ship called *The Ruys*. It was manned by a crew of Dutch officers and Indonesian ratings. It was a cross between a luxury liner and a cargo ship. The officers had the first class accommodation, and all the rest had hammocks slung below decks in what must have been the holds when the ship carried cargo.

We cadets had been told that we would be given a certain amount of privilege on board, while in fact we were fairly low down the decks, and most of the army fatigues were put on to us. I daresay it did us good, as it was about the only experience of service in the ranks that we were to get.

There then began a seven week voyage from the Clyde to Bombay, going right round the Cape, as the Mediterranean and Suez were not to be used.

We travelled in a convoy of seventeen ships, escorted by two Royal Naval vessels, and I suppose we moved at the speed of the slowest one.

On the first morning after embarkation we found ourselves out in the North Atlantic, we assumed we were going round the tip of Northern Ireland. Life on board the troop ship soon settled down to a fairly regular routine.

We did life-drill exercise on our first morning afloat, but our main routine was doing such things as a short spell of P.T., hearing a few lectures and, most important of all, our instructions in Urdu or Hindustani, the chief official language in India.

As we were due to be commissioned into the Indian Army this was a 'must' for all of us officer cadets. For me personally this presented no difficulty, for having come straight from school and being rather good at languages, I found this new course of study quite easy-going. We were all issued with a little handbook of Urdu, and I spent hours up on deck in 'free time' working through this book well ahead of the set instructional lessons. By the time we got to Bombay I was able to converse a little with Indians in their own language.

II

Landing and Disembarking

After several weeks at sea we put into the port of Freetown, Sierra Leone, West Africa, or rather we lay offshore. We were there for four days, mainly in order to refuel and revictual the ship, but there was no going ashore for any one.

Some of the local inhabitants rowed or swam out to our ship and entertained us by diving in the water for pennies and such like thrown overboard for them.

We caught a glimpse of an African village, but it was rather maddening just having to sit tight on board. Needless to say, in typical army fashion, the daily routines of P.T., lectures, fatigues, study, all went on unabated, just as much as when we were on the move.

Eventually the whole convoy set sail again and we went on without incident until we got to Cape Town about two weeks later. Here also we stayed for four days, but with this difference: we went right in to harbour to re-provision and on each of the four days almost all the troops were allowed to go ashore for several hours on their own. This really was rather nice, and made a pleasant break in the long, weary voyage.

The local South Afrikaners were very obliging! It seemed to be the 'done thing' for families to pick up enlisted men and to take them for drives or into their own homes. One such family took charge of me and took me for a drive into the National Park, then to their home for a meal and into town for a film, before depositing me by the dock gates in time for going back on board.

On the second day ashore I was more on my own. I had lost some money on board, stolen I believe, and did not find things easy. But I managed to get up to the Rhodes Memorial gardens at the top end of Adderley Street, and then up in a cable car right to the top of Table Mountain - overlooking

Table Bay on one side, and the Afrikaner hinterland on the other. This was a truly magnificent sight. The cable car had crept to the top rather falteringly, and I had thought it was going to go crashing down the valley at one awful moment. But we got to the top all right, and back again.

We had been warned beforehand of the existence of the Colour Bar in Cape Town. This did not affect us deeply at the time, but one saw with disgust the notices on buses, railway stations etc - the signs of enforced segregation: Whites only; Coloureds only, and so on. I was not very much impressed with all this one way or the other. I was only 18½, had just come away from a single-sex boarding school, where segregation of a different kind had been practised, and politics, race relations and the like meant little to me as yet, though I was to become interested later.

We had another day ashore at Cape Town when I wandered around rather aimlessly, having spent all my money, and no further kind South African family offered hospitality this time. But these days ashore were a very welcome break in the monotony of the voyage.

After the last day, when the last drunken soldier had staggered back up the gang plank, we set sail again on the final lap of our seven week voyage, and did not see land again until we came to Bombay.

Here we were quite quickly disembarked and had to march to a 'Rest Camp' on the city's outskirts for a stay of three days.

We were addressed by an old ex- Sergeant Major type colonel sitting astride his horse, the Camp Commandant, who said he was nicknamed 'Old February' because as a penalty he always gave 28 days C.B. (confined to barracks).

As we were not to be under his command for anything like that length of time anyway, we did not see how his remarks could possibly apply to us. But we had to listen to his strictures about camp discipline all the same.

A few of our draft were detailed to mount guard over the rifles and bayonets that we had brought with us, quite unnecessarily, from London. I was not selected for this irksome duty but had a few hours off that evening.

From the camp gates I caught a bus into town and tried out my faultless Hindustani on the bus conductor who persistently refused to understand me, though I am quite sure that he did so really. I was soon to learn the strange truth that 'educated' Indians somehow felt it a matter of shame to be addressed in their own langauge, and were proud only when they could be spoken to and reply in English.

When I got into the centre of Bombay I made straight for the office of the Commissioner of Police, because I had an uncle who was Deputy Inspector General, Criminal Investigation Department, in Poona. Mr Butler, the big police chief of Bombay, kindly received me, put through a telephone call to my uncle at Poona, and invited me to dinner at his house on Malabar hill that evening.

After some hours wandering about the town, I duly presented myself at his select residence, and was entertained in splendid style by himself and his wife. What I remember in particular about this visit was the fact that one took Indian servants for granted, and when, all too anxious as usual to try out my Hindustani, I thanked the waiter for serving me at the meal, I was told that it just was not the done thing to attempt to thank servants!

An Indian driver from this illustrious household drove me back to the camp gates. There was one way in which I could have thanked him, and that surely would not have been spurned, by giving him the customary 'backshish' or tip. But as I had no money on me, I shook him by the hand instead, to his great amusement!

III

From Bombay to Bangalore

After a day or two more at the camp, we were to move out to board a troop train for a three day journey to South India.

We took leave of the good British officers who had been in charge of us since we left London, and were taken under command of Captain Taylor of the Staff of the Officers' Training School Bangalore, who had come up from there especially to escort us. He gave us a few instructions far less tersely than 'Old February' had done, and then began our train journey. This was fairly uneventful, though not without interest. We stopped regularly at certain stations for receiving of rations, but had been forbidden to buy food or drink from the Indian vendors who thronged most stations. Once again I had the opportunity of trying out my Hindustani. One vendor asked me through the window where I thought the train was going to. I told him that I did not know, but that I thought it was going to go via Poona. It was then his turn to shake me by the hand, and to express his thanks.

I thought afterwards that perhaps I had given away secret information to a potential spy! But I was prouder to have communicated successfully in the local language at last!

Sure enough the train did go through Poona in the middle of the night, and during the stop there I received a letter from my uncle, delivered by his own servant, who somehow or other sought me out from amongst the ranks of all the cadets. I managed with the help of another cadet to give him a 'backshish', with which I hope he was satisfied, and then away we went again.

Eventually we drew near to our destination, Bangalore, in Mysore State. It was supposed to be on a plateau and to boast a mild climate, but it seemed quite warm enough.

On arrival we were greeted by the 'School' Regimental Sergeant Major, who ordered us sharply to unload those 'bloody' kit bags; and then we were taken in vans to the Officers' Training School. This was supposed to be the Indian equivalent of the British Sandhurst.

Strangely we were supposed to be treated as 'officers and gentlemen' there, and yet at the same time the staff of British N.C.O.s who were to instruct us, obviously enjoyed bellowing at us and making us 'jump to it' while on parade, knowing full well that we were soon to be officers. There was almost a split-minded approach in the treatment of us. We were addressed as 'gentlemen' by our officers, and as cadet number so and so by the non-commissioned officers.

But on the whole it was a pleasant change to be received at this comparatively comfortable establishment after weeks of being pushed around.

We were shown to our quarters, two to a 'room' or floored tent. I shared one with a cadet called Mike Prossor, whom I had scarcely met before, and we had an old Indian servant to wait on us.

Our first meal at the Officer Cadets' mess was marvellous for its good fare in a comfortable building, and being waited upon by white-coated Indian servants.

The next morning we were woken up early, by our servant with Chota Hazri, or 'little breakfast', which preceded the main breakfast, for as a rule we were to do about two hours work or training between the two. I don't think we did very much on our first full day, which I believe was Sunday. But we all had to go along to the 'Shop' run by a Contractor called Shan Sher Din, who had the monopoly of selling the necessary to the cadets.

We were supposed to purchase certain 'essential' additional items of uniform from him, plus a complete set of athletic gear some of which I still have to this day. So perhaps the old rascal was not so bad. But at the time I hotly resented being commanded to buy this, that, and the other. The athletic gear was for evening exercise, as if we had not had enough in the day already!

A typical day at the O.T.S. Bangalore was something like this:

We were awakened at dawn by the old servant. We washed and dressed and went out on parade. We were usually pushed through the 'assault course', which included jumping, clambering, crawling, with full kit, and, hardest of all, climbing up ropes hand over hand, and trying to get down again without tearing our hands. It was not too bad. I don't think we ever had live ammunition fired over our heads as we crawled across an open space with heads well down, as had been threatened.

We then had a pause for a decent breakfast at the Cadets' Mess.

After that our main morning session of training and instruction began. We always had one daily 'Urdu' lesson, with an Indian 'munshi', or langauge instructor to two or three cadets. I was or thought I was, well ahead of the official course by this time.

We might later be out on Weapon Training, or Drilling, or Map Reading, or being lectured on organization and administration. Sometimes we used to cycle to our training point which may have been a few miles out. Then the whole platoon or company would move off in military fashion, 'prepare to mount - mount!'. And off we went in twos on our cycles, in as orderly a manner as possible, until the order 'Prepare to dismount – dismount!' was given.

We would return to base for the midday meal, a comfortable affair in near officer style, and recommence training in the afternoon. We even had an afternoon tea break at the mess, when we were again suitably regaled, if we wanted to be. (The old rascal in charge of the mess, used to sell off those cakes which cadets did not care to consume, but was most reluctant to produce more if any of us wanted more than our ration!)

In the late afternoon or early evening we were supposed to do compulsory sport, hockey or basketball or something, and most of us did so.

Then, after a bath and change, there was dinner in the mess, all in fine style, and I think we usually were tired enough to retire to bed soon after that.

That of course was a typical ordinary day. There were exceptions to this kind of routine. Sometimes we would be out on an all-day exercise, with packed lunches and water bottles and none of the comforts of the mess. Sometimes it was the other extreme and a special mess-night was held, when all cadets were to be present in good order, and an officer presided at the formal toasting to the King-Emperor.

IV

Training at the O.T.S.

The entire course at Bangalore O.T.S. lasted five months for my lot, and six for others. At the time of joining, one had been given two choices, of opting for one of the 20 Infantry Regiments of the Indian Army, or for the R.I.A.S.C. No other branch of Service was offered. For some reason I had got the idea that the P.B.I. (Poor bally infantry) was dull, not dangerous, and had put my name down for eventual commission into the Royal Indian Army Service Corps, and had stuck to that. Looking back on it, I think that the Infantry had much more to offer. On the other hand, I might not have survived. But I was not motivated by such thoughts at the time. The basic course of training was the same, except that those destined for the Infantry did the full six months, and those of us for the R.I.A.S.C. did only five, October 1942 till early March 1943.

Some of us had been together since London. At Bangalore we were joined by a number of genuine Indian officer cadets who, like ourselves, were being trained for becoming King's Commissioned Officers in the Indian Army. Relations with them were on the whole easy enough, and although it was the custom to talk English in the mess, and English was also the language of the parade ground, some of these brother cadets could help us with our Hindustani. Their Hindustani was of the top grade, while we were supposed to learn colloquialisms enough to be able to talk to the troops over whom we would eventually have command. This put me properly in my place, and left me more confused than ever as to whether it was good to be proficient in the language or not.

This dichotomy of language also led to one or two amusing incidents.

An English sergeant was once drilling a group of us and commanded us: 'From the right, number!' An Indian cadet being at the end of the row began in his own language, and was followed by the others - 'ek, do, tin, char.'

Then it all had to be repeated in English - one, two, three, four.

Some of the instructing sergeants were not so decent as ours, and used deliberately to mispronounce the Indians' names to taunt them.

Once one staff sergeant was reprimanded by the Brigadier Commandant for being too hard on the 'cream of the English youth', to which he retorted: 'Well, all I can say, sir, is that the cream has gone sour!'.

To assist us in our training there was stationed nearby one Gurkha platoon for demonstration purposes. These men really were marvellous. It gave one a thrill of pride to see these little men come on in perfect marching order, and when carrying out an exercise, all their movements were precise and superbly harmonised, performed with the minimum amount of words of command. They certainly showed us how things should be done.

Towards the end of our course we were all sent out on a mammoth cross country run, and I recall with pride finishing 18th out of about 600 contestants.

The final testing piece, near the end of the five months was a 'whole day exercise' and camp followed by a route march back through the night.

We had quite a tough day out in the sun, after bivouacing the night before, and then began the 17 mile long march back to the O.T.S. We marched for an hour at a time, with a five minute pause each hour to sit down in the ditch and take a small swig at the water bottle which we all carried, but which was not supposed to be refilled. A truck followed to pick up any stragglers who might fall out, but I remember that of my particular training platoon we all made it. No one fell out on the march.

As we approached the 'School', one of the cadets remarked that he looked forward to ice creams in town the next day when we knew we were going to be free; to which our officer gruffly commented that a pint of beer would do us much more good. That exchange shows just how 'raw' many of us were.

Not long after this lists were posted of those of us who had successfully completed the course and were to be commissioned as 2nd Lieutenants into the R.I.A.S.C. as from a certain date. My room-mate Mike Prossor was staying on the extra month for the infantry, but I wasted no time in buying an officer's tropical uniform, with peaked cap, and baton, and brown boots etc.

Then I had a proud moment. In just about my first hour as a young officer I passed one of the toughest sergeants who had been drilling us before, as he was riding on his bicycle. He immediately stiffened his arms in the form of a salute, which I acknowledged, I hope, in the proper manner.

The incident was significant, however, for it showed army etiquette at its best. As long as we were cadets, it was the sergeant's job to shout at us and toughen us up. But as soon as we became officers, they showed the respect that they customarily showed to *all* officers of whatever rank.

It might appear that those of us who received our Commission early, were 'stealing a march' on those of our comrades who had another month to do. But in fact, although we were gazetted as fully commissioned officers after five months' basic infantry training, we were to have a further three months' course as officers at the Service Corps' own training school right up at the other end of India, at Kakul, in North West Frontier Province, up Khyber Way.

the form of a salute, which I acknowledged, I hope, in the proper manner.

The incident was significant, however, for it showed army etiquette at its best. As long as we were cadets, it was the sergeant's job to shout at us and toughen us up. But as soon as we became officers, they showed the respect that they customarily showed to *all* officers of whatever rank.

It might appear that those of us who received our Commission early, were 'stealing a march' on those of our comrades who had another month to do. But in fact, although we were gazetted as fully commissioned officers after five months' basic infantry training, we were to have a further three months' course as officers at the Service Corps' own training school right up at the other end of India, at Kakul, in North West Frontier Province, up Khyber Way.

V

Up to N.W.F.P. and more training

Our journey from one end of India to the other was to prove most instructive. We were to learn quite a lot about the life of the real Indians, and the comparison between their lives and those of the British overlords who, just about literally, lorded it over them.

It was invariably the custom for all the British officers and senior civilians to travel first class by rail. A first class compartment consisted of two main seats, and two pull-down bunks up above. Thus four usually travelled in one compartment, for journeys were often up to four or five days, and one lived and slept in the carriage. There were organised stops for meals at stations which had Refreshment Rooms, and here the 'Sahibs' were waited on with the utmost servility. For example when the scheduled time for departure drew near, instead of an immediate blowing of the whistle and raising of the green flag to go, the guard would come along respectfully to the senior officer in the Refreshment Room and ask if the 'Sahibs' were ready to resume their seats on the train so that it could set off again. If they were not quite ready, well the train would wait until all the superior folk were ready!

I was to go on several long journeys like this during my sojourn in India.

On this first journey as an officer I remember that we set forth from Bangalore to Madras on the first leg of the route, and then on up through Central India to Delhi. As we rolled on through the vast unending plains, I was struck by the overall sameness of it. One could go mile after mile, and still see very little change in the dull, dry, hot, earthy plains. There were some exceptions, of course, but this was the dominant impression that I got.

We stopped in Delhi for a day, and this was an opportunity to see the capital, especially to see the rather fine New Delhi. Two or three other new young officers and I took a horse-drawn cab, rather like an Irish jaunting car, and were driven round the main show parts of the capital. We saw Vice-Royal Lodge, modelled on Buckingham Palace, a triumphal Arch modelled on the Arc de Triomphe of Paris, and the Parliament buildings modelled on the Roman coliseum; and we travelled the full length of Connaught Place - a fine main street possibly comparable to Princes' Street in Edinburgh.

In the afternoon we saw something of Old Delhi and the 'Lal Yila ', or old Red Fort.

When we returned to our train we were ready for our next lap. The journey was far slower than it need have been, but no one seemed in any hurry. As we approached the North-Western Frontier the scenery did seem a bit better, and the appearances of the local inhabitants, who always swarmed around railway stations, were less swarthy than down south.

After another night we stopped at Taxila, a most interesting place, which was supposed to have seen the march of Alexander's Legions. We had a whole day there, and wandered into the Museum which was quite a gem.

As always, we were pestered by poor peasants who seemed convinced that every Sahib was a rich man, and whose one idea was to try and persuade him to part with his money.

Eventually the train was allowed to proceed. Quite why it had been held up so long we never really discovered.

We arrived at the nearest station for Kakul, our destination, after dusk, and it took some time for trucks to come down from the R.I.A.S.C's School to collect us all.

The number one priority there seemed the allocation of 'bearers' or Indian servants, whom we were more or less obliged to engage for not too high a fee, and who came to clean our boots and belts etc. and look after our clothes. For an officer to do such things himself would have been quite 'infra dig'.

Each officer had his own room here, instead of sharing, as at Bangalore. The messes were quite nearby, and the fare was generally good.

There then began again our life on a training course which was fairly routine once it got going. Although by now we were indeed officers and were paid as such, we still had to do the occasional drill parade. Our main job, however, was to learn all about S. & T., Supplies & Transport, the main business of the Service Corps.

The Supplies side of the course was mainly receiving lectures about the intricate accounting system, which had to be kept up even in wartime. The Transport side was more lively and involved outdoor work to a greater degree. D. & M., Driving and Maintenance, came in to it in a big way. We were supposed to learn all about the construction and functioning of the internal combustion engine, though it would be unlikely to fall to us as officers actually to handle such things personally.

Similarly we were all supposed to become proficient at driving army 15 cwt and 3 ton vehicles, though once on service were not expected to do so. The officers' job if in command of a Motor Transport Company was to sit in front of the leading vehicle beside the 'sipahi' driver, with map case, compass, and binoculars ready to hand, commanding the convoy on the move. He should not drive unless his driver was shot dead! This rule was not invariably obeyed, but still was supposed to be in force.

We did plenty of driving during training, however. Once we went out with a civilian driving instructor beside us, on an unfenced mountain road, by night, and with only dimmed side-lights! Passing this test successfully I think subsequently well qualified us for anything we might have to do in connection with driving ever, for what could be tougher? Two or three times during the course we had a two or three day 'exercise', when we were out camping with field rations, and practised the combination of Supply and Transport.

One rather amusing incident took place towards the end of the course. A couple of young British officers, not, I hasten to add, members of our batch, had disgraced themselves by insulting a senior officer at a hotel at the nearby town of Abbotobad. For this they were both put under close arrest in their quarters, and they had to have one officer each of our group to be quartered with them and to act as escorts until the time came for their Court Martial.

When it came to my turn, which was almost the first day of their house-arrest, to perform this particular melancholy duty, another officer and myself did our best to comply with our instructions and to maintain reasonably cordial relations with the 'prisoners' in our care. They were allowed their daily exercise, and used to take a vicious delight in walking their escorts as far as they could in the midday sun.

The funniest thing, however, was when one of them went to call on a friend of his in a nearby hutment to inform him that he was under arrest, and then, as an afterthought, on deigning to recognise my presence said, 'You haven't met old ball and chain, have you?!'

Soon after this incident our three month course came to an end. It was now June 1943. I do not recall that we were examined, but on completing our training were now ready to go on into real service.

We had joined to fight the Hun and the Jap, and were indeed to be sent shortly to an operational area against the latter, although the job of the Service Corps, although fully armed and equipped, was not primarily to hunt down the enemy.

VI

First Posting and First Assignment

My posting, together with that of several others, when it came through, sounded very inconspicuous. It was to report to the officer in charge of another Transit Camp at a god-forsaken place called Gaya in Bengal. But it was obvious that this was only an intermediate position and that we were bound for the Eastern frontier.

First began another long three or four day train journey. We were given ten days leave before reporting at Gaya, and I had time to get down to Poona for just three days' leave and visit my Uncle who was Chief of Police there. He resided at the magnificent Club of Western India together with other Senior Civil Servants and the like, where everything was very 'pakka' and tip-top.

I enjoyed my short break before beginning my real service. I then proceeded back via Bombay, up through Central India, bound for Gaya. By this time I had rejoined some brother officers both British and Indian, who were all bound for the same destination. Gaya proved to be rather a drab place, as we had been led to believe. We had virtually nothing to do there, but several of us, including some who had been with me from the start, after three days were ordered to report to the Commanding Officer No 5 Supply Company at a place called Gauhati in the Province of Assam. Off we set again by train to Calcutta, only to be told by the R.T.O. (Railway Transport Officer) that we could not proceed further for another three days. We were quartered at a lodging-house in that teaming city of millions. We saw about a bit, but thought it not nearly so fine as Delhi or Bombay.

Then we could go on again, *and* this time by a very narrow gauge line up into Assam, and by ferry across the great Brahmaputra river. At least we got to Gauhati, but that was still not the end of the road for me, scarcely even the beginning. We went to another Rest Camp for a further day or two, and were beginning to be split up further, when the adjutant of the Supply Company to which I had been posted arrived to collect me and one other young officer and take us to headquarters. Even there they did not seem to know quite what to do with us, and it looked as if they had to rack their brains to find a suitable job for us to do. Ultimately I was told to go on another lap of a journey, to report to Lieutenant Alcazar, officer in charge of a Field Supply Depot at Digboi up in North East Assam. After interminable delays, I eventually got there. It was up in the heart of the tea-planting country and there was a big oil depot there, owned by Burmah-Shell, I believe.

Mr Alcazar, who had just been promoted to captain, seemed flabbergasted to see me. He explained that his unit normally had only one B.O.! (British Officer, full King's Commissioned Officer, whether English or Indian), in his strength, and that I was already super-numerary. This really was too much, after all my travels! However, he received me quite kindly, gave me a tent to live in, and allowed me to share his 'mess' with him – which was just about what it was, for it meant eating in his rather untidy office – and told me I had better under-study him, and try to learn how an F.S.D. operates. He took me to call on the manager of the big oil depot in the obvious hope of getting an invitation for both of us to his house and club the first Saturday evening, which was sure enough what happened; and a few days' later he drove me in the only vehicle attached to his depot to call on a tea-planter, who also received us socially.

On our return to the supply depot we found that another young fledgling officer had joined to report, a 2nd Lieutenant Morgan. This was too much for Lieutenant/Captain Alcazar, and really drove him 'up the wall'. To have one young officer thrust on him unexpectedly was bad enough, but two!!

He began frantically telephoning Supply Company HQ 100 miles away, Area HQ at Gauhati, Sub-Area HQ somewhere else, anywhere to relieve him of this by now unwanted influx of new young raw officer material.

His efforts and exertions seemed to pay off, though perhaps not in quite the way that he had expected. 2nd Lieutenant Morgan was unfortunately attacked by malaria and had to be admitted to the Indian Military Hospital nearby, and I, after a few days, was ordered, not to report to someone, *but to take command of* a D.I.S. (Detail Issue Section) at Jorhat in Southern Assam.

At last I was to do a real job. I set off by night with a rail warrant and got down to Jorhat sometime the next day. I turned up at the office of the D.I.S., after enquiring the way from the station, and confronted a humorous Scot, Lieutenant Thompson, from whom I was to take over. I knew very little about the handing over and taking over procedure, but he was kind enough to instruct me. But first he had to fix up where I was going to live. He had been living at the house of an American missionary, Dr Cooke, who lived quite comfortably very near. The good doctor agreed to take me in too. I forget the exact arrangement. I am sure I must have been a paying guest, but was certainly quartered at his house.

Later that day, or perhaps it was the next, Thompson and I did all the checking of all the Stores in the Sub-Depot, and the handing over/taking over documents were prepared by an Indian 'babu' or clerk for our joint signatures. So thus I had my own command. It was but a detachment or part of a Supply Section under the command of another Lieutenant which operated a Field Supply Depot at a place 10 miles away by road. But still I was on my own.

Usually one had a V.C.O. – Viceroy commissioned officer to assist one. These gentlemen often described as the backbone of the Indian Army, were in a way comparable to N.C.Os in the British Army, except that they were half-officers, being entitled to salutes from Indian Other Ranks, but not from British Other Ranks. Furthermore there was a whole array of Indian N.C.Os answerable to them as well.

I think my next senior soldier was a Hawaldar or Sergeant, together with Several Naiks or Corporals, Lance Naiks or Lance Corporals, and ordinary 'Sipahis'. This was my staff to operate the Sub-Supply Depot on the site of what once had been a match factory. We held tons of supplies in sacks and boxes, and fresh food supplies were delivered daily by local Indian contractors. They were supposed to submit tenders for the best bargain as long as the end product complied with army specifications, and I had a bit of a job sorting out these gentlemen. But I managed somehow.

We had several hundred if not thousands of troops, both British and Indian, dependent on us for their rations. Their quartermasters had to come in daily for the fresh supplies, the others being 'drawn' for longer periods at a time. Everything had to be accounted for, down to the last ounce, even at the height of the war, otherwise the Auditor-General would be down upon us, and sometimes he was too.

There was a rigid scale of rations for both B.T. (British Troops) and I.T.

(Indian Troops). We were supposed to supply exactly the right amounts authorised to be issued, and of the right quality. We were supposed to hold 30 days stock of non-perishable items, and if we looked like running low, had to indent for more.

The units dependent on us came in daily with their individual ration indents, and our very efficient clerk deftly calculated the right amount for each, then I signed the Issue Order to the store-keeper of our main 'Go-Down' or store-shed, which was the authorisation that counted. If anything went wrong, I would be held responsible.

Actually things ran, or appeared to run, fairly smoothly. One thing we did have to be very careful of, however, was this. To the Hindu the cow was sacred, to the Moslem the pig was unclean. No matter, to neither of them was beef or pork issued. But they were absolutely insistent before receiving fresh mutton that the sheep or goat had been killed in their prescribed manner; for the Moslem it was necessary to issue Meat Halal i.e. that the animal had been killed by having its throat cut; for the Hindu it was necessary to issue Meat Jhatka, i.e. that the animal had been killed by one swift blow on the head! The army fully upheld and endorsed this rule. Any mix up of this kind would have resulted in the most dire consequences - a Second Indian Mutiny maybe!

Things still went along quite well until the arrival of a huge American unit at Jorhat to take over an air base there. To our surprise they wanted to be on us for rations, and expected everything to be in high-class order. A huge American truck arrived to collect rations just when the amicable Indian contractor was delivering fresh supplies for all. 'Get that God-damned thing out of here!' roared the Master-Sergeant! Little did he realise that he could not get his Requisition fulfilled unless he gave way at the main entrance. I believe he did give way, eventually, but day after day from then on his vast truck drew up, and sometimes nearly got stuck in the mud.

The arrival of the Americans had its social implications also. There were both white Americans and Negroes in the big Air Corps unit stationed nearby. Some of them came round to see the good Dr Cooke, with whom I was billeted, and of a Sunday evening he would hold a 'social' for any Americans who cared to come, usually ending up with some magnificent renderings of Negro-Spirituals, rendered live, by some first rate American negro soldier singers. All this helped to liven up proceedings.

Life went on at the depot quite steadily for months. I was in command there for five months, August to December 1943. During that time my promotion from 2nd Lieutenant to Lieutenant came through, this was supposed to be semi-automatic after six months, but I had to remind the authorities about it.

Then one day I heard from the Adjutant of Supply Company Headquarters at Gauhati that a new Headquarter Company was moving in to take over. I asked not to be moved, but he told me in a semi-official letter that I was already under the new command, and that it was entirely up to the new Colonel whether I went or stayed. As I suspected, my days there were numbered.

A little while before, I had been visited by the D.A.D.S.&T. of our Sub-Area – Deputy Assistant Director Supply & Transport. He, a major, had come into my office, and had treated me, a humble Lieutenant, with a most magnificent salute. It was the custom when visiting officers in their own commands to render such courtesies. The major expressed himself entirely satisfied with his visit of inspection, which gave a big boost to my morale.

But it was different when the new Colonel arrived a little while later, flanked by several supporting officers. He gave me the most cursory of salutes, and then began to find fault with my organisation. What finally incensed him, however, was the fact that I could not lay on lunch for him and his entourage. It was too much for Dr Cooke to entertain so many. So they had to be content with the local Chinese Restaurant!

The party left, slightly disgruntled.

I feared the worst, and sure enough the blow soon struck. I received a Posting Order to Company headquarters itself at Dibrugarh, another big tea-planting centre. A young Indian K.C.O. came to relieve me, who did not want the comforts of Dr Cooke's house.

The good doctor and some of his negro guests sang 'God be with you till we meet again' on the final evening there, and away I went by night again up to the North of the Province to report for my new duties.

VII

From Assam to Bengal

It was just before Christmas 1943. My new duties were not very onerous, regimental duties at Company HQ, the Colonel called them, which meant assisting the adjutant and supervising the work of the 'Sipahis'.

One was even permitted to have some social life. But what did rather irk me was the fact that the Colonel seemed to want to put the young Subaltern (myself) firmly in his place, dining in correct order of precedence etcetera. All the officers of his staff lived in a long low bungalow type of building directly opposite the local 'Club', built and sponsored by tea planters in palmier days. If we were told to attend a social function there, we went. The Colonel apparently considered it part of the training of the young officers, even though it was well into the middle of the war, and I had already held my own independent command.

At one of these functions I met Madge Montagu, the beautiful daughter of a local tea planter, with whom I fell madly in love, only to discover that she was already married! I met her at several dances, and even called at the Montagu residence on a few occasions where I was made quite welcome.

Anyway fate soon put an end to any nonsense, for after a few weeks we were again on the move. The Supply Company H.Q. was itself ordered to be removed from N.E. Assam to South East Bengal, nearer the Burma border. I went with them, and we went by train down to Chittagong. We stayed there a few days and then moved on with all our equipment such as it was, down the long, hot, dusty, Arakan Road which led from India into Burma. Here we were in a Field Service Area, classified as operational, but technically known as L. of C., Lines of Communication, well in advance of base, but not quite front line, though near enough. We encamped at a jungle green place called Ukkia, until the high command decided what we were supposed to do.

It was here where I had my nearest experience of action. A report came through that the Japs had broken through 20 miles behind the lines, and might well be in our vicinity. I was ordered to take a small party of men out by night to look for them! We were instructed to don gym shoes in place of army boots so as not to give away our position by the cracking of twigs if we trampled on any. Like all officers I was armed with a pistol, and the men had rifles and bayonets. We were out for several hours but found nothing. I don't know to this day how we would have reacted if we had come face to face with the enemy!

We got back to camp at daybreak, when the Colonel decided to call the whole 'exercise' off. The adjutant ordered hot tea with a splice of rum in it. Never had drink tasted so delicious as at that early hour and after our near encounter with death.

Soon after this I was sent to a place on the sea called Cox's Bazaar, a few miles back, to check the loading and unloading of supplies coming in by sea.

After a few weeks there I was sent to a Field Supply Depot at a place called Oltakali to assist the Indian captain in command there.

By this time I was well and truly fed up with being shunted around. I decided to apply for a transfer, which I had every right to try, and, rather to my surprise, my application was accepted.

VIII

Work at the Advanced Base Supply Depot

At last I was going to be doing something useful again. I was posted to No 6 Indian Advanced Base Supply Depot, at Nutenpara outside Chittagong. This was a vast Store Holding Depot, which had a vital job to do in the war effort. I arrived there on June 6 1944, D Day for the Allied Invasion of Normandy.

I was to be there for another year. The Commanding Officer was a kindly man called Colonel Smailes who had been one of my instructors at the R.I.A.S.C. School at Kakul, earlier.

I was allotted a 'bacha' hut made out of bamboo, and dined in the 'bacha' officers' mess. We listened to the news over the radio in the ante-room until the light faded.

The next day I took command of No 591 Indian Supply Section, operating C Sub-Depot of the vast Base Depot. I had an Indian V.C.O. a Jemadar as 2nd in Command, and had a team of educated N.C.Os as store-keepers assisted by ordinary Indian sipahis and some civilian 'coolies' who were engaged daily. They were quite a good bunch.

I had a certain amount of administrative work to do in the 'daftar' or office, plus getting around to the 30 odd store-houses in my charge, each holding about 200 tons of supplies on average. Again we had to be very careful with accounting, but were concerned with holding huge stocks, not with any direct issue to troops as had been the case at my first command.

The Colonel let us get on with the job, and did not interfere as a rule, but was there in the background to be referred to if necessary. He took a genuine interest in the welfare of his officers and men, and was a most efficient Senior Supplies officer besides. He was my idea of what a Commanding officer ought to be. Unfortunately he was moved on, probably promoted very deservedly, fairly soon after my arrival.

His successors were not quite so good, either being of the ex- Sergeant Major type, or emergency commissioned officers like myself. Colonel Smailes was a regular Indian Army officer of the best type.

My brother officers were quite decent, both British and Indian.

The men under my command were quite a happy crew. There were Hindus, Moslems, Sikhs, Christians, and men from all over India.

This was a pleasant feature of the R.I.A.S.C. In the twenty Indian Infantry regiments they were nearly all of one class, race, or creed, which I suppose may have made things easier. But I can't say that we had any particular difficulty on this score.

One of my duties was to hold 'Orderly Room' at Section HQ. Offenders were marched in to be summarily dealt with by their officer commanding. Officers below field rank (major) could award up to seven days imprisonment.

One poor fellow had overstayed his leave by a few days. For this he was supposed automatically to lose pay for the number of days absent, with the addition of any penalty thought fit.

I was no sadist or power-lover, but it seemed to me that the sipahi deserved the maximum that the law allowed. I awarded him 'Sakht Din Sakht gaidi', seven days rigorous imprisonment, which meant that he had to stay in the Guard Room and help lift boxes like the coolies.

All officers were supposed to be well versed in Indian Military Law. It was part of our training.

During my service I had to sit on numerous Courts of Enquiry, and take down 'Summaries of Evidence' in the vernacular (Hindustani) but this instance was the only time that I had to dish out so severe a penalty.

I related earlier how sensitive Indians were to matters of their religion, particularly as it affected food. As a rule they did not mind handling B.T. rations in store, but occasionally things went wrong.

We were supposed to hold a fixed amount of stocks of all items, but it seldom worked out exactly. Sometimes things had been too long in store and we could not get them passed on to the ultimate consumer.

If tinned food went bad, the only way to account for the loss was to get a Medical Officer's Certificate that it was 'unfit for military consumption', the implication being that though not good enough for the fighting troops it was still all right for other kinds of humans! It would have been very wrong, however, for any of us to have sold such goods in the civilian market. After being thus 'condemned', that authorisation was sufficient to allow us to strike off the amount of goods from the accounts, and the actual bad goods themselves had to be dumped in a great big pit outside the Depot's boundaries. They were then 'deemed' to have been destroyed.

When it was tinned milk it was not so bad. But when tinned bully beef went bad, it presented a problem. The coolies were with the greatest of difficulty persuaded to load the offending crates into lorries to be driven away to the dump, and then to destroy them. The stench was bad enough for anyone, but must have been harder for those who earnestly believed the cow to be sacred. They all put kerchiefs around their faces, and the driver and store-keeper were willing to convey the unwanted possessions to their final resting-places. They looked like a gang of dacoits up to no good, and the sight of them was ridiculous, but one pitied the poor fellows in their plight.

At another time at the height of the rush, goods came pouring into the railhead which was in the centre of the Main Depot. The goods were unloaded there by coolies answerable to a Railhead Supply Detachment commanded by a captain. They were swiftly reloaded on to tip-up lorries. Now normally these would come around to the appropriate store-shed in the Sub-Depot, to be correctly counted and receipted. But when the pressure was on, the drivers were ordered to use their tip-ups and thus to decant the stuff in the roadway in front of the 'basha' built store-shed. With sacks of sugar, flour, or rice and the like, it did not matter so much. But when flimsy crates of tinned milk and tinned fruit were thus deposited, it meant instant loss. This near criminal wastage which clearly defeated the authorities' own purposes incensed me, and I tried to give orders that it should not happen. But the Major who was 2nd i/c of the A.B.S.D. and his Stocks Officer insisted, and I was powerless to resist. The new Colonel kept well in the background.

IX

Sickness and Leave

It was now over a year since I had had any leave. The usual quota was one week in three months, or four weeks in a year. I put in for the full ration, which was granted. I got as far as Calcutta when I suddenly went down with malaria, fortunately of the 'Benign Type', but still quite serious enough if not treated promptly and correctly. I was admitted to an Indian Military Hospital, where the course of treatment to combat malaria was quinine, meppacrine and pammocrine, administered in that order. Then all patients were suddenly evacuated by Hospital train to Secunderabad in Hyderabad State in South India.

When I was discharged from there I was granted sick-leave, and so was able to proceed on my way to my original destination before I had succumbed to this quite devastating illness. I was aiming for Madras, which was not so far away. There I went to stay with R. Hill-Turner, a senior official of the Madras and Southern Mahratta Railway, who was the father of a school friend of mine. I stayed a day or two with him at his comfortable cool bungalow.

Then he sent me off to join his wife and little daughter at their summer house up in the Blue Nilgri Hills, the most delightful part of South India. I travelled overnight to Mattapalyam, the railhead or end of the line, and then up by a quaint ricketty old Indian bus climbing up the hills, to Kotagiri, which was a charming spot, quite like an English village.

The climate was extremely mild, and the scenery very pleasant though not majestic, so different in both respects from the hot, dusty sandy plains which seemed to be the dominant feature of much of the mainland of India.

My hostess received me kindly and it was quite like living in an English family home again. There was a local Club for the Sahibs, to which most of the tea planters and officers on leave resorted. Frequent dances were held there, and it was there that I first met and fell under the spell of Astrid Selling, a gorgeous creature of 18, the daughter of a Swedish Match Magnate. I was but 20, and there were a number of young officers falling over one another to dance with her. I met her a few times, and a year later was to see her again at the other end of the Indian subcontinent.

While staying at Kotagiri we visited Oatacamund, the show-piece of the Nilgris, yet not quite so attractive as the smaller place. After about two weeks, the family with whom I was staying decided to return to their main home in Madras, and I went with them. My leave ration had not yet expired, and I had a further week with them at their home. Then I was required to report to a medical officer before being passed fit to return to my work. This being satisfactory, I took leave of my good friends with whom I had passed such a pleasant 'leave', and set out on yet another of those long four to five day train journeys across India.

It was on this occasion when the custom I had reported earlier of the British overlords being waited on by the guards was seen most pointedly. A certain green-jacketed Colonel, returning to his unit in Burma, made the train wait until all the officers had had an unhurried meal. We got back to Calcutta, and eventually I got back to my unit at Chittagong.

X

Return to Chittagong

I had been away so long, what with my term in hospital and extended sick-leave, that they had almost forgotten about me, but not for long. I was allowed to resume command of my own Section and of C Sub- Depot of the Base Supply Depot, and more or less picked up the traces from where I had last left them. During my absence, I believe another British officer had temporarily looked after the Supplies side of things, while my V.C.O. and 2nd in Command, Jemadar Mangat Ram, had looked after the men. He soon put me in the picture as to the good service and 'peccadilloes' of some of the members of the section, and we resumed our cordial relationship and good understanding. Only once did we have a misunderstanding when I addressed him in his own tongue, Hindustani, and he was very put out!

During training it had been impressed on us that the mark of a good officer was one who took a deal of trouble over the welfare of his men. I think both he and I tried to live up to this, and it was a happy partnership.

Perhaps I should explain that whereas the Indian Infantry was broadly similar in organisation to that of the British, in the 'Rice Corps' as the R.I.A.S.C. was not inappropriately nick-named, a Supply Company was roughly equivalent to a Battalion under a Colonel's command, and a Supply Section, normally a Captain's or Lieutenant's Command according to seniority and length of service, was equivalent to a Company in the Infantry.

We continued to operate the Depot with no major incident for months.

The men, as I have indicated, were a pretty good lot. Occasionally temptation was too much for a Store-keeper or maybe some of the coolies, and one would find a hole cut in the corner of the vast bamboo store-shed in which the more precious food items or 'Hospital Comforts' were stored, and a few bottles missing. We could not find the culprit, and there were far more serious losses through over-stocking and things going bad through lack of regular turn-over. The men had little to entertain them, but went stoically on.

When the time of Ramadan came on, when all good Moslems would not eat or drink anything from sunrise to sundown, some of the most zealous Moslems from Hawaldar to Sipahi tried to carry on with their work with this self-imposed discipline on top. One could not but admire this stern self-control, and the fact that some of my men were of such calibre more than attoned for the petty foibles of others of them.

For myself the principal hardship was the climate which was very hot and sticky, but better than the 'dry heat' of the plains when one could not even perspire freely.

The officer was indeed in a privileged position over all. He had his tent, and his batman, and the relative comforts of the Officers' Mess. We were about mid-way between the base, where those stationed at such places had the comforts of a peace-time station, and the frontline troops who were exposed to the full rigours of climate and enemy action. We were technically on the Lines of Communication, classified as being in a field service area, or on active service, without being fully operational.

Occasionally a truck would take some officers into Chittagong for an evening. Once we went on to see the famous actor Noel Coward perform with some E.N.S.A. folk, especially for the British officers and men in that area. He began to sing the song about 'Mad Dogs and Englishmen, who go out in the Midday sun', and then he came to the line 'In Bengal, to work, is scarcely ever done at all'! - This really brought the house down; (except that we were out in the open!) for we all worked like dogs day in and day out, in supporting the war-effort.

Such ventures out were on the whole few and far between.

Life in the Depot continued fairly evenly. Christmas 1944 came along and the war in Europe was progressing well. For a day or two we had some easing of work, and celebrations in the Mess, but no extra leave except for those for whom it was routine.

In February 1945, when I was just 21, my promotion to Captain came through, though I still continued, and was quite happy to do so, as O/C 591 Supply Section Operation & Sub- Depot of 6 I.A.B.S.D.

Soon after this time the British Government announced its intention of abandoning its ten year party truce (for there had been no fresh Parliamentary elections since 1935) and of having a General Election. Serving soldiers overseas were to be allowed to have a postal vote, and I was supposedly eligible to vote. Unfortunately my application for this did not get through in time.

In May came the wonderful news of the end of the war in Germany, and the final surrender to General Montgomery on Luneberg Heath of all the German Land Forces. We got the news over the radio. It all seemed very far away to us.

We were in an area which had first been termed 14th Army under Field Marshal (later Sir William) Slim, also known as 'The Forgotten Army'. About this time it became absorbed in a greater area called South East Asia Command, under Lord Louis Mountbatten as Supreme Allied Commander.

As we were in business mainly to defeat the Japs, V.E. or Victory in Europe Day, did not mean so much to us, but meant on the other hand a 'hotting up' of the war in the East.

An all out drive was made to bring this war to a speedy conclusion, though official opinion thought that it would take a long time yet, as indeed it might had it not been for the unexpected later.

The emphasis was now on Air Supply. We were drawn quite closely into this, although we did not see the results of our labours.

While earlier the big matter was to get vast supplies stocked into the Depot, as quickly as possible, the important matter now was to send special packed supplies out, known as 'K' Rations, in big quantities, and quickly. In order to accomplish this, a 24 hour round-the-clock work rule was established, with officers and men working on day and night shifts alternately. At the same time routine supplies had to be received in, and 'orderly room' and other administrative work had to be fitted in also. We managed somehow, but quite a trying time it was, with the hot, sticky, climate, and the dull hard slog of a rather inglorious but nonetheless very necessary kind of work to be done.

XI

Another Leave and a Long Journey

In the month of June, a year after I had first joined the A.B.S.D., between VE Day and VJ Day, I got my next year's month's leave. I had thus twenty-eight days, but it was going to take me ten days travelling to and from the place I wanted to get to, giving me 18 days there. I had an ambition to visit Kashmir, the beautiful Swiss like mountainous province of Northern India, but what drew me there more than anything else was that I knew that Astrid Selling, who had cast such a spell on me on my previous leave, was staying up there at the Nedous hotel at a hill station, Gulmarg.

I set forth on the long journey across the plains, via Calcutta, Delhi, to Rawalpindi which was the railhead where the line ceased. From there one had to travel a further 200 miles by car up into the heart of Kashmir.

Finally one had to go on foot with the help of Indian bearers to carry one's kit up into the pine trees of the place we were aiming for. There were horses and donkeys up there, but no mechanised transport.

I managed to get into the one rather fine hotel run by a Norwegian with Indian assistants. It was quite expensive but well worth it.

I lost no time in calling on Astrid, who received me quite graciously, but it was obvious that I was not the exceptionally favoured one.

I danced with her, and went out riding with her too, but so did other officers, and if I had expected to be singled out, I was sadly mistaken. One day I went climbing with another officer on leave. We went up a manageable mountain above the Pine trees until we came to the snows. There was a view across to 'Nanga Pavna', Bare-Breast white mountain in the Himalayas.

My fortnight up at this mountain resort was very pleasant, apart from feeling a bit love-sick. There was a Club to which all officers on leave were instantly admitted as temporary members. Golfing, riding, walking and climbing seemed to be the main daytime pursuits. Once the Vice-Roy was to

The Life of an E.C.O. in India

broadcast and the Secretary of the Club went round vainly trying to persuade all the officers to attend, most of them were not particularly interested!

At the end of my leave I returned by the same route - no overstaying through sickness this time - walk back down the hillside, car to await me at the foot to drive back to Rawalpindi, then the long train journey across from N.W. to N.E. India with the usual meal stops etc.

During the return there was a stop at Lahore for a few hours - the capital of the Punjab, and now one of the principal cities of West Pakistan.

I went around in a horse-drawn vehicle, and saw some of the fine buildings of the British lords in their heyday.

Eventually we got back via Calcutta and so to Chittagong again.

XII

End of War in the East

The tempo of life at the Depot now was one of feverish haste, in the all out drive to chase the Japs out of Burma with the help of troops operating well ahead of base, who were dependent on us for the promotion of air supplies. I resumed my job immediately this time, and fell into the routine of day and night work alternating again. It was quite tough going. Not nearly as hard as for those in the real frontline, but still we were doing a real job towards winning the war.

I caught malaria again, and was admitted to the Indian Military Hospital in Chittagong. There was no means of telling whether this was through a fresh mosquito bite, or a recurrence of the original bout of it. It made little difference anyway. I had the by now familiar treatment, and then was discharged after about a week to resume my work and duties.

We were really working flat out in the Depot now, and expected a continuance of pressure for some time.

Then one day in August, we heard that the war in the East was over, that Japan had decided to capitulate after the dropping of a few atomic bombs over their mainland. We never expected this sudden collapse, of course. I first heard the news from a young Indian K.C.O. who came singing round my quarters in the evening - 'Hurray the War is over.'

A few days later the Colonel ordered a Victory parade for all the officers and men of the A.B.S.D., which was rather poor in comparison with general military standards, as the men were not of the smartest, and had had virtually no parade ground drill since their training. At least they had been doing their allotted job.

Then in the mess that evening the Colonel made each officer tell a joke or sing a song in turn. One Sikh Major told the Indian servant to tell the British Colonel to '--- off', but the Indian servant was too sensible to pass the message on literally.

The war was over, yes, and the pressure was off. But the emergency period went on for another 18 months or more, and clearing up operations went on all over the Far East. Much was to happen before final demobilisation.

XIII

Home Leave

Soon after the official end of the war I had an unexpected change.

There was being formed a new Force called B.C.O.F., British Commonwealth Occupation Force, and this was to go to Japan. My own particular Section, No 591 Indian Supply Section, was earmarked to join this force. I myself was destined never to get as far as Japan, but it was some honour that the particular unit which I commanded was selected for this venture.

The Base Supply Depots went on functioning, and no doubt another Supply Section from somewhere was found to operate C Sub-Depôt. But my own band was baled out on a certain day in September 1945, and proceeded with all personnel, stores and records etc. to travel across India from East to West to a Camp at Nasik, North of Bombay, where the various units which were to comprise B.C.O.F. were assembling. Months were to elapse before the eventual departure of the Force by sea from Bombay. We had no idea that it was to be so long.

In my own case I had applied for home leave some while before.

My move away from South East Asia to Western India did not invalidate my chances of getting this.

One day in November word came through that my application had been granted, that I was to have 28 days leave in the U.K. by being flown home for it.

Accordingly I left my unit (a new young Indian K.C.O. took over from me), and I went to report to the Air Transit Camp at Poona, not very far away.

Although at this stage the getting of home leave was for some a fairly routine matter, there were others at the Transit Camp who had a far stronger case - men who had been wounded in fighting, and repatriated prisoners of war.

I was very lucky to get this U.K. leave 'ration', especially as I had had my full quota of local leave in India as well. On the other hand there was this aspect to it: emergency Commissioned Officers like myself had been recruited in Great Britain, and were guaranteed free passage back to the home country if we survived! At the same time, as long as the emergency lasted, India was also our home base and we were liable to further overseas service from there.

Anyway I found myself on this draft of British officers and men bound for U.K. We, about twenty-four of us, were put on a Dakota plane of R.A.F. Transport Command, and were flown first to Karachi, in North West India, later the capital of West Pakistan and the whole of Pakistan. Within a few hours we were on our next 'hop'. We had six of these, of approximately six flying hours each, but at some of the intermediate stops we had quite a long halt.

Our first halt was at Bahrain Island in the Persian Gulf, where we stopped for a meal. Then on again to Habbaniyah in Iraq. Here we had a night and a day pause. It so happened that my cousin, formerly an officer in the W.A.A.F.s, and her husband were stationed here, and I won't easily forget the look of amazement on my cousin's face when I almost literally dropped out of the clouds and descended on her. I stopped at their house for a meal and spent the evening, and then returned to the air posting camp.

Some time the next day we were off again, and this time to Lydda in former Palestine. We were 'held' there two days. We learned to our dismay that previous drafts during their two day halt had been taken round to see the Holy Places of Jerusalem and Bethlehem, but as some riots had been going on, this privilege was not accorded to us. (It was about the time when the British Mandate over Palestine was coming to an end, and independence for Israel was foreshadowed, but was not yet a reality).

Our next stop was at El Adem, by Tobruk, in the middle of the night, but a meal had to be eaten if we wanted any, for nothing could be served aboard the 'plane.

Our fifth and final stop before home was at a small airfield in Sardinia where again, we had a meal, and then the last hop of six hours.

The flying was a little uncomfortable. I dozed off much of the time. Some of the company who were more alert told me that flying over the Alps had been scaring, because it appeared that we were dangerously near some peaks. I expect this was deceptive, and am sure that the pilot knew what he was doing, even though it was an old 'plane.

The only unpleasant part of the flight to my mind was when we seemed to swoop down rapidly which caused a painful sensation in the ears. Sometimes in mid-air we would hit an 'air pocket' and lose height rapidly for a few seconds, which was a bit sickening. But on the whole, it was a good journey, though nothing to compare with modern jet flights of course.

At length we crossed the Channel over 'Old Blighty', and landed at a small air station called Broadwell outside Oxford.

Later that afternoon, I think it was a Saturday, we were taken in by truck to Oxford Station, Great Western Railway, were given railway warrants and on to London. Then we had to go to another Transit Camp, a converted London hotel in Knightsbridge, and finally were given 'warrants' to our homes or desired places of leave.

I got down to Orpington, then in Kent, now part of the London borough of Bromley, at about noon on the following day, and was met by my parents.

I had not seen my Father for five years since he had been overseas before I went out to India, having the distinction of being a volunteer officer in *both* world wars. My Mother I had last seen just under four years before.

I had a pleasant time back at home. It all seemed rather small, and unreal, until I got used to it. But it was not my final homecoming, only a short leave.

Things were going quite well, and I was quite prepared to return to duty, when I went down with jaundice just before Christmas and had to be admitted to a local civilian hospital which had a military wing. This was rather a bore. It meant an extended leave, also a loss of some army pay. One compensation was that I met a rather attractive nurse named Lorna O'Brien whom I took out a few times during my convalescence.

About the middle of January after going before a medical board at the India Office in London, I was passed fit to return to duty but was recommended to go by sea and not air.

I reported to the same London District Transit Camp where I had originally joined the Forces three and a half years before, but this time, of course, as an officer, and received rather different treatment, except that the same rather brusque Commandant was in charge still. He objected to being told what to do about us by the India Office. 'The War Office runs things in this country', he tersely commented.

XIV

Return to India

About the middle of January 1946 a batch of us officers returning to India were taken to Waterloo, thence by train to Southampton where we boarded the *Cape Town Castle*. This was a fine ship of the Union Castle Line. Although supposedly a troopship it was in very fine condition. How different it was returning to India this time, when automatically and freely first class accommodation was provided for all the officers. We had cabins of four, and dined in the magnificent dining room at the purser's table, being waited on by stewards, and being regaled with quite sumptuous fare.

There was quite a mixed bag of us on board - many officers like myself returning to the East after leave, including even a few ex- P.O.Ws going back again which seemed a bit hard; an E.N.S.A. troupe to entertain the Forces; some ladies of the W.V.S; and some civilians, all enjoying the first class fare. Below decks but not nearly as grimly quartered as we Cadets had been on our former outward journey, were some British troops, and some Italian Prisoners of War being sent home. They, poor devils, sat huddled together, mostly rather seasick in the early days out at sea.

Our route this time was to be different too, naturally enough; no long trek round the Cape in Convoy, but calmly entering the beautiful blue Mediterranean and later to go on through the Suez Canal.

Our first stop was off Gibraltar on a sunlit afternoon. I wanted so much to be able to go ashore, but the O.C. Troops, a Wing Commander, was unrelenting and would not allow even the daughter of the Admiral of Malta, who was among the civilian first class passengers, to go ashore to see her friends. Instead the Flag-Lieutenant from Gib. and another companion came on board our ship to see her, and paced the decks for an hour or so. Then back they went by lighter, and away we went up into the Mediterranean.

A few days later we anchored off Valetta, the main harbour of Malta, and stayed a day or two to refuel and re-provision. But again no going ashore for anyone. It was maddening - seeing these wonderfully interesting places, but not being permitted to set foot on them.

Our next stop was at Naples. This was mainly to take the Italians home. A sad sight here was seeing an Italian wife or mother stand at the gangway, and scanning all the men as they came ashore one by one, and then going away weeping, because her man was not among them.

Again one longed to visit Napoli or Naples, but it was no good, even though we were not laying off but had come right alongside the harbour.

We weighed anchor one evening, sailed past the volcanic island of Stromboli, and on into the wide open sea again.

The next piece of drama occurred as we approached Port Said and the entrance to the Suez Canal. We lay off there for a few hours, and then entered the Canal shortly before nightfall. The next morning we were out past Ismaelia, and then out in to the hot Red Sea, with glimpses of Sinai across the other side.

Our last stop before getting back to India again was off Aden. A small party was put ashore, and some Indian soldiers were taken on board. But we did not go right close in. I don't think we missed much, but at all the possible stops we were thwarted in any hopes we may have had of going ashore.

At length after a voyage of about three weeks we put in to Bombay. Again how different was our arrival from that in the height of the War. An officer from port embarkation came on board within minutes of our tying up alongside, and addressed the officer class in the First Class passenger lounge about the arrangements for disembarking.

Most of the officers who were unattached like myself, meaning not directly in charge of troops at the time, went directly ashore and to the main railway station to travel to a Rest Camp a few miles out. This was rather a grim place with not a tree in sight. For some it was their first experience of India. For myself I was quite glad to be back, though never at any time from the moment of joining onwards, had I any serious intention of staying on. I regarded it all as a fine interim experience.

The time now was March 1946, and the newly instituted Labour Government had promised independence for India either as one country or, in the Partition principle, as two. There were certain signs of unrest and growing excitement, but the army routines carried on unabated, and so, as far as one could judge, did civilian government besides.

I doubt very much whether I could have stayed on, since the new Indian army was to be completely Indianised, with only a few English officers staying on as advisers. But it would have been possible to transfer to the British army for a regular commission, or to stay on in India in some civilian capacity, had I so wished.

After a few days I was instructed to report to The D.A.D.S.&T. (Deputy Assistant Director Supplies and Transport) at Poona. My former unit had by this time left for Japan, and there was no serious question of my rejoining them, nor did I particularly wish to. My uncle too, whom I had visited at Poona in 1943, had left the Indian Police in 1944 and had gone to live in South Africa.

XV

Two Postings

My reporting here was thus purely incidental. I stayed at an R.I.A.S.C. officers' mess for a few days, until a regular posting could be found for me.

The job that I was then to take up proved to be quite a pleasant one, I was to proceed to a Station Belgaum, to the South of Bombay and Poona, in the heart of the Mahratta country, where one of the crack Regiments of the Indian Infantry had their Regimental Headquarters. But my task was to assume command of the Station Supply Depot there.

I took over from a British Captain, in charge of all the supplies, and command of the V.C.O., N.C.Os, and men who constituted the depot's staff. It was a pleasantly appointed place, and operated more as a peacetime station, though was still supposed to be on a wartime footing.

I could have lived in the depot, but was persuaded to 'mess' at a joint officers' mess for officers of the R.A.M.C., who operated a hospital and R.I.A.S.C. a few miles out. This meant that the driver of the truck attached to the depot had to ferry me out every day. It was more like keeping office hours. The V.C.O. was prepared to assume responsibility in the evening time. There were few parades or formal occasions. I was answerable to the Area Headquarters in Bombay for Service Corps technical matters and for local administration to the Administrative Commandant of Belgaum.

This was not a difficult job, but simply required steady application and thorough administration. I was largely left alone from up above, and was supported by an able band of men and a particularly good V.C.O. as 2nd in command.

As in the real wartime days, representatives from the various units dependent on us for supplies came in every day to draw their fresh rations, and once a week for their dry rations. All had to be strictly accounted for. The wartime system of accounts operated, but this seemed to be fairly thorough.

By this time I was well used to Supplies, which meant dealing mainly in food. The R.I.A.S.C. was also responsible for the provision of P.O.L. (Petrol, Oil, Lubricants), and big stocks of these were held in our depot. I knew little about this side of things, though was nominally responsible for the lot, but fortunately had a very good N.C.O. in charge of this section who looked after things well and who always insisted that visiting officers should hand over their matches to him at the moment of entering the P.O.L. Section!

What would have happened had the whole thing gone up in smoke I shudder to think, but in the hands of such a capable young man this eventuality seemed unlikely, and fortunately did not happen.

As always at Supply Depots we were supposed to hold stocks of thirty days plus reserve for all the troops in our area. In this respect we also had a most unusual rôle to fulfil.

There was, at a place called Kohlapur, some miles to the north west, a camp which housed about 600 Polish refugees. Although they were not daily dependent on us, we were supposed to hold reserves for them in the event of their being cut off by the equivalent of Civil Rights disturbances in the latter days of the struggle for independence or the like. I was constantly receiving letters from higher authority about this special scheme labelled 'asylum', not because the inmates were insane, but because they had sought political asylum with the British in India! I was repeatedly being asked to furnish evidence that we held the necessary reserves, as a matter of top priority. I was also urged to go out to this camp and to see for myself.

At length I decided to act on this, and leaving the V.C.O. in charge as I did every night anyway, I set forth with my driver doing a duty round to get to Kohlapur. There was a retired Colonel in charge, a kindly old man, but the camp was mainly full of women and young people. I could not but admire the spirit of these folk who kept on with little hope of returning to their homeland. They had fled from the Germans, and by now the country was overrun by the Russians. I never discovered their eventual fate.

I recall having a brief tour of inspection of the stores under cover which seemed in reasonably good condition, having a meal in their canteen with the old Colonel ending with tea and lemon in the Slav style, and a conversation in English with a particularly pretty Polish young woman.

I would like to have done more for her and all her compatriots. But there was little that I could do, and before I might have occasion to go again I was removed to a different posting.

We returned, sobered, late at night, the driver depositing me at the mess from which he had picked me up in the morning, before returning to his depot. I had had a whole day of duty without going near the depôt.

By far and away the biggest unit on our ration strength was the Mahratta Regiment. Their Quartermaster Sergeant used to draw vast quantities until we suspected that they were over-drawing. A staff officer from Sub- Area HQ then came down to investigate the matter, and directed that they must not 'hold stocks' like a miniature supply depot for themselves, but simply requisition according to their actual ration figures.

Once, reminiscent of former times, a sipahi of my unit returned late from leave, and when I ordered his pay be stopped, he demanded to see the Colonel, which was his right.

As the nearest RIASC Colonel was over 100 miles away, we had to make do with the nearest Colonel on the spot, who was the 2nd in Command of the Mahratta Regiment HQ, a Colonel Harrison. He saw my recalcitrant sipahi, who was a bit of a 'barrack room lawyer', in my office, and reduced his sentence by half. He then confidentially recommended me to get the man posted away as soon as I could.

Relations with the Mahrattas were very cordial. I was invited to a social at their magnificent mess, which my duties at the depot precluded me from accepting.

There was some social life on the Station, however. There was a Club, to which all officers could belong if they wished, and a squash court attached to it. I used to exercise myself there not infrequently.

There was a very nice girl called Daphne Alexander, the daughter of a Forestry Inspector, who was also a member of the equivalent in India of the A.T.S., whom I met occasionally, but as she was the only white girl on the Station and much admired by most of the Mahratta officers, I did not stand much chance with her.

Suddenly one day, quite out of the blue, and with no warning nor apparent explanation, a posting order came through for me, just when things seemed to be going along so well. I smelled something suspicious about this, and my sense was not misguided, but there was little that I could do about it. I telephoned through to Area HQ in Bombay mildly protesting, but there was no mistake as to the authenticity of the order.

In fact there had been some 'pulling of strings' behind the scenes. In due course an Indian K.C.O. arrived to take over from me. He freely admitted that he had got this posting on compassionate grounds in order to be near his family who lived near by. This was fair enough, but we guessed that he had friends in high circles.

As he was a family man, he did not need my quarters. We completed the necessary formalities for handing over and taking over, and then I proceeded back to Poona where I had been instructed to report.

XVI

Poona and Simla

I found myself back among old associates some of whom I had known during training at Bangalore and Kakul. I was to work at the Main Supply Depot, which was a fairly sizeable organisation commanded by a Major, with a number of officers responsible for various workings of it. My particular job was to assume command of a Railhead Supply Detachment which was a Captain's command.

In wartime organization the proper function of such a unit was to receive stores coming in by sea or train, and then, after checking, despatch them further by Motor Transport or even by Animal Transport Companies in hilly country to their eventual destination. We had come across one at the A.B.S.D. at Chittagong, and I had worked alongside one at Cox's Bazaar even earlier.

But at Poona in the heart of peacetime India, this seemed scarcely necessary. Anyway, orders were orders, Poona was indeed quite a congenial place to be stationed at, and matters might indeed have been worse. So I set to work with a will.

I tried to infuse some sense of pride into the detachment which appeared to have been growing slack recently before. I suppose this was understandable. The war as such was well over. Some of the men, like their British counterparts, were eager for their discharge. And the educated ones among them were probably looking forward to Indian Independence besides. The time was now July 1946.

I lived at a general officers' mess for the R.I.A.S.C., one had closed down since several of the officers both British and Indian were family men. I had an office at the Main Supply Depot. The men were quartered nearby. Most of the work was done at the railway siding outside Poona station, and I went down every day to check at least once. Goods, destined for the Depot, came in by rail, and had to be unloaded by coolies, checked by an Indian N.C.O., and receipt for the whole consignment had to be signed by the officer responsible. Similarly outgoing goods had to be despatched by us with great care. One of our recipients was my former happy Depot at Belgaum, and often enough I checked the seal on a wagon destined for them. Unfortunately this was not foolproof. From time to time goods would be received at either end not in the condition in which they had been despatched, due either to theft, negligence, or even unavoidable delays on the line. It was very difficult to attach blame and responsibly in such cases. The army was responsible for correct accounting, and losses in transit were not readily admissible. If criminal responsibility could be pinned upon any sipahis or railway officials it would be, but this was very difficult to establish. Sometimes some of them were in error, at others it was difficult to attribute blame to anyone.

We kept on our daily routine without major mishap for some time.

I was assisted by a very enthusiastic Sikh N.C.O. named Subedar Shan Sher Singh. A Subedar was one higher than a Jemedar in the hierarchy of V.C.O.s, the highest being Subedar Major.

The Sikhs were an interesting people as a race or religious sect. They all wore their turbans by day at all times, from officer down to the humblest sipahi. I had come across some before, but working in close conjunction with one of them taught me more about them.

Poona was all right to be in though not as great as it must have been in the really high days of the British Raj. There was a feeling that things were running down, as the forthcoming independence of India, with Partition as it turned out, were foreshadowed.

I was not rich enough to enjoy the high society such as the hospitality of the Club of Western India where my Uncle of the Indian Police used to reside. And it was not 'done' to fraternise with the local Indians too much. If I went out at all it was for a meal at the Chinese Restaurant and cinema to follow, or such like.

This particular posting at Poona looked like lasting quite a time, as indeed it did. My turn for being repatriated and demobilised was not due for at least another six months. Inevitably one had thoughts, if not anxieties, about what was to happen when one did get eventual discharge.

Some civilians tried to persuade me to stay on in India, which might not have been such a bad idea. Back home there would be lots of people seeking civilian employment at about the same time, but to do anything worthwhile one would probably need further training.

People such as I who had gone straight from school to officers almost all too easily acquired an inflated idea of our own importance. Certainly we were being paid far more than young people in civil life in England would be getting when just starting their first jobs. As a Captain, overseas, I was being paid about 600 rupees a month or approximately £600 a year.

The idea of the big drop and starting afresh did not appeal exactly, and some E.C.O.s of my acquaintance were in favour of 'deferring' their release for a further six months or so, thus cashing in a bit longer on the good pay and conditions, but probably only postponing the evil day.

Being uncertain as to my ultimate career except that I wanted to do something useful in civilian life, I 'hedged' for a bit longer.

There was a scheme for training officers to be Senior Civil Servants and administrators which appealed to me, and for which I decided to apply. This involved going up to Simla, the summer capital of India, for an interview.

This in itself was an interesting experience. I quite easily obtained leave of absence for about five days in order to make the journey up and back. I travelled up by the B.B.& C.I., Bombay, Baroda, and Central India Railway and back by the G.I.P., Great Indian Peninsular Railway. The last part of the route was along a narrow gauge line climbing up the Himalaya foothills. This was quite fascinating. Simla, reminiscent of Vice-Royal Lodge, Kipling, and Empire, was a fine place in its heyday, although already beginning to fade a little.

Scenically it did not possess the grandeur of Gulmarg in Kashmir where I had been on leave the year before. Nevertheless it was still quite impressive. I stayed 24 hours at a hotel, had my interview with a Senior Civil Servant and a non-committal result, and then began the long descent back to the plains and the longer journey across the plains back to West India.

XVII

Disbanding of a Unit

I have already mentioned the atmosphere of a slow 'running down' which seemed to pervade the army and civilian government in India. It was, almost literally, the decline and fall of the Indian Empire.

For the poor average native, tilling his soil behind an ancient plough, and scratching a living from the soil, I don't suppose things were in the least different nor yet many years later. But the feeling of anti-climax after the war, coupled with the presentiment of imminent change, was certainly prevalent amongst the British and amongst the educated Indians of whom we had not a few in the Service Corps.

I was shortly to be present at the demise of a unit. Following the policy of cutting down, whole units were sent to be disbanded en bloc. Some of the men could re-enlist, but many did not. My unit then, No 4 R.H.S.D, 4th Railhead Supply Detachment, was ordered to proceed in its entirety with stores and equipment and records, to Ferozepure in the Punjab, N.W. India, which was the R.I.A.S.C. Centre for raising units and for disbanding them. I had not been with them for long but as I was still in charge, I had the slightly melancholy task of taking them up by rail to the north in November, in order that they might be disbanded.

We arrived at Ferozepure early in a morning, slightly cold it was, unusual for India, (though it could get hot enough in the middle of the day). There we stayed for about three days, while the unit's records were checked, and each man had to have his own personal records, pay books etc. similarly checked. Then, apart from those who wanted to continue service, they were given warrants back to their homes. Some were sad to quit the Service, and were almost in tears, particularly a few ordinary good-hearted sipahis.

The situation reminded me of American negroes being set free from slavery, and, not knowing what to do with that newly found freedom, begging to be taken back! When, fortunately, the records and so on were found to be in order, I got my own first class warrant back to Poona, and reported again to the British Major in command of the Main Supply Depot. The duties of R.& D., Receipt and Despatch, which still had to go on, were taken over by an ordinary Supply Section, or part of one, attached to his depot, and a job for me had to be found.

I was given the least glamorous of all, while still retaining my rank of Captain, I was diverted to take charge of the Central Ration Station of the Depot, dealing simply with the daily issuing of fresh supplies to Units in the area. This was not a very stimulating job, but one which still had to be done. There was little point in applying for a transfer at this late stage when my own turn for demobilisation was not far off, so once again I set to as well as I could. The hours of work were much the same as before, and I continued to live where I had been recently living. It was not a particularly satisfying kind of work, as it was not an independent command, and the men working with me were drawn from various Sections, or some just loosely attached to the Depot, so it was not a really genuine unit to look after. But still we all did what we had to do.

An amusing incident followed to liven things up a bit. As in Assam at the height of the war against the Japs, daily contractors had to bring in fresh supplies. These were supposed to comply with R.I.A.S.C. Specifications, and nothing but the best was considered fit for military consumption. At the same time if the contractors tendered offers that were too expensive, or their wares did not come up to standard, then one was not supposed to accept them.

All I could do was to apply the law as I understood it. On Christmas Eve 1946 the British troops in our area came to draw rations. They were supposed to be given special Christmas Fare, i.e. turkeys and geese as meat ration instead of mutton or beef. The Contractor was unable to supply the right amounts at the right time, or they did not come up to specification, and so the ration drawing quartermasters went away, slightly disgruntled with ordinary rations only.

But that was far from being the end of the matter. They must have protested to their unit commanders, who in turn complained to the Brigadier commanding the District.

Sometime in the evening, when I was sitting quietly in the Mess, a staff

The Life of an E.C.O. in India

officer came round enquiring for the Supplies Officer. I guessed I was the one, and we had to drive round to the residence of the Brigadier who reprimanded all concerned, unit commanders as well as supply people, for not taking action earlier, but directed that, come what may, the British troops must have their Christmas special rations. Accordingly I had to go round in the night to the local market, where there appeared to be quite a hive of activity, and buy up after all from one of our regular contractors, enough turkey, chickens, etc. to feed all the British troops dependent upon us. These had to be conveyed to the depot, and the unit vehicles came out in the small hours to collect them.

It seemed to be a matter of top priority that nothing but the best should be issued to the troops. Always fresh supplies were to be issued if available, second best was tinned food, and third substitute was dehydrated. It was rare not to give them best.

Once much earlier on in the height of the war, during the 'push' from Assam into Burma, I had been ordered to get an Indian Field Bakery, attached to my Supply Section to work through the night on preparing hot-cross buns for the troops. This to me seemed the height of absurdity, and I had expressed amazement and utter incredulity at first. But there was no mistake, and we had to go ahead and get it done.

Truly the Service Corps' job was to serve!

This incident, however, in Christmas 1946 was based on the same logic no doubt. I had been threatened with dire consequences for not enquiring in advance that the troops all had their due, but as I was about to be repatriated very shortly I was not in the least scared by the fire-breathing Brigadier.

However during Christmas Day an Indian bearer came round to my bungalow bearing a note from the Colonel who was 2 i/c to the Brigadier, informing me that no further action was to be taken and that I could enjoy Christmas and the season of goodwill. This was very decent of him, though, as I say, at this time I was not particularly worried about the outcome.

XVIII

Home-coming and Becoming a Civilian

Early in the New Year of 1947 I had to decide whether to defer my release or to accept repatriation and demobilisation when it was the turn of my own age and service group to have it. I decided to accept.

I had a quick visit to Bombay to arrange about despatching heavy baggage through Port Embarkation. I had another quick visit down to Belgaum to check on the correct arrival of goods that had been sent down to them from Poona. I even got an invitation to the highly exclusive Club of Western India where the Senior Civilians used to live, through a police officer who was nearer my own age.

But it was clear that my service was about to terminate. The men of the Central Ration Section held a small party in my honour, and then I left my last command and went to join the other temporary British officers who were about to go home to U.K.

For all this there was a clear procedure. One had to go to Deolali, near Nasik, to the north of Bombay, which was famous for being an Artillery Centre, but which also housed the transit camp through which all officers bound for U.K. had to pass.

We were there for a few days dealing with documentation etc, and then went by train to Bombay prior to embarkation. So far things had worked fairly smoothly with the minimum of delays or hitches. We embarked on a converted liner to troopship which had been originally called the *Empress of Japan* and owing to the war had been rather foolishly renamed the *Empress of Scotland*.

I left India with mixed feelings. I never really wanted to stay there, but had grown to like some aspects of the life there, and especially some of the people as individuals.

I also knew that, apart from the good luck of surviving the War, in a sense, 'we never had it so good', for officers were a privileged class, and all were well paid. Of course one might easily not have survived.

The people back home had been exposed to worse dangers through bombing than ever I was. But I might just as easily have been sent to the front line against the Japs, and been shot or captured. My war had not been a glorious one, but hard work had been done and we had certainly 'served'.

As our band of about-to-be repatriated emergency commissioned officers gathered on board, it was interesting to see a fair number of those who had originally joined with me all going home together, having converged from various parts of India and the further East. Most had elected to come out at due time, and a few gave news of others who had decided to stay on. I don't recall hearing of one who had been killed in action, but it may well have happened. All had had different experiences. Some had had the short home leave, eighteen months before, as I had. Others had gone right through the full four and a half years, 1942-1947, on full service. Most of these brother officers seemed in good shape.

The average rank attained by any of us, was Captain like myself: a few had got to Staff Captain or Major, one young man had even been a temporary Lieutenant- Colonel.

The voyage back home was undramatic. There were fewer ports of call than on the last voyage, but I doubt if there would have been any going ashore even had we stopped.

We did not call off Aden, went through Suez by night, and had quite a long pause at Port Said. One concession here, however, was that Egyptian traders were allowed to come on board to hawk their wares, and one made a few purchases of leather goods, like wallets and handbags with pictures of the pyramids clearly marked on them. But that was all the contact we had with Egypt. That was also the last stop or port of call. We sailed on up and through the Mediterranean, no looking in on an Italian port or Malta this time, but we did have another glimpse of Gibraltar, where the straits are so narrow that one can see well, even though we did not lay off, as on the journey going out.

So on out into the bleak Atlantic and across the Bay of Biscay.

We were not informed precisely as to which English port we would be going into, but at length we discovered that it was to be Liverpool.

On a bleak day in February 1947 we came to the first lifebuoy off the Mersey, and then on up the estuary to Liverpool docks.

For some officers and men on board it was their first sight of 'Blighty' for several years. It was not a particularly brilliant home-coming. England was undergoing a spell of seven long weeks of snow, in which the sun hardly ever seeped through. And Liverpool was not exactly a beautiful place to which to return. But here we were, the end of our service, and the future lay ahead.

Of my main narrative, there is little left to relate. We disembarked that same day, and went on by train to London, except those whose homes were in the north. There was no need to go through another centre for documentation this time, but I could carry on to my home in Kent, only fifteen miles south east of Central London.

One further duty or privilege remained, and that was to travel down to Woking in Surrey a few days later there to receive a complete civilian outfit of clothing. It was not the best tailor made stuff, was very much the same for all, both officers and other ranks, but it was nonetheless quite welcome as clothing was short and was also on ration.

I was still on the strength of the army for a few weeks more, and was entitled to wear uniform if I chose to, on fully paid up leave.

My official date for discharge was 14 February 1947, exactly four years and a half from my date of joining. I was given a 'gratuity' of £80, and four medals from the Commonwealth Relations Office, which had recently taken over from the India Office. These were the 1939-45 Star for service on the first part of the War; the Burma Star for 18 months service in the Burma border; the Defence Medal for 3 years continuous service overseas; and the War Medal which *everyone* in the Armed Forces on VE Day received, from the highest Field Marshall, Admiral or Air Marshall to the humblest Private, Rating, or Aircraftman, whether one had served right through, or whether one had just joined a Service.

I was then just 23 years old.